Most drones fly but many remote
controlled machines are also called
drones. This *Minidrone Jumping Sumo*
can make spectacular jumps – and film
the action as it happens.

DRONES

Henry Brook

Illustrated by Adrian Roots, Giovanni Paulli and Staz Johnson
Designed by Helen Edmonds and Anna Gould

Edited by Alex Frith
Drones expert: Dr. Mirko Kovac, Aerial Robotics Lab, Imperial College London

This Puma drone can fly through the air almost silently. Soldiers use it in live battle zones to see what's behind enemy lines.

Contents

This is a *Predator B* drone. It is half the size and a fraction of the weight of an F-16 fighter plane.

These pods contain extra fuel, to allow the drone to fly missions that last over 36 hours – far longer than a manned aircraft.

What are drones?

Drones are robot vehicles that carry no human pilot or driver. Most drones can fly, either by following radio commands from a pilot on the ground, or using on-board sensors and computers.

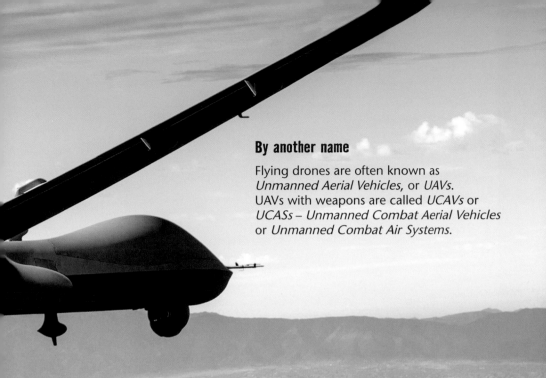

By another name

Flying drones are often known as *Unmanned Aerial Vehicles,* or *UAVs.* UAVs with weapons are called *UCAVs* or *UCASs – Unmanned Combat Aerial Vehicles* or *Unmanned Combat Air Systems.*

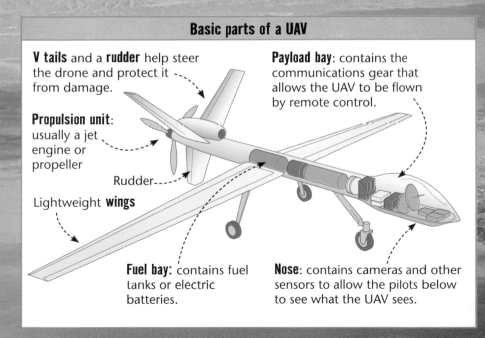

Basic parts of a UAV

V tails and a **rudder** help steer the drone and protect it from damage.

Propulsion unit: usually a jet engine or propeller

Rudder

Lightweight **wings**

Payload bay: contains the communications gear that allows the UAV to be flown by remote control.

Fuel bay: contains fuel tanks or electric batteries.

Nose: contains cameras and other sensors to allow the pilots below to see what the UAV sees.

What can drones do?

Most drones are used as flying scouts, providing images and information from battlefields, storms, busy cities – even distant planets. They can also operate on land or underwater, tackling almost any job imaginable.

Eye witness

Drones can get in close to follow and record with no risk to their pilots.

- sporting events
- movie stunts
- natural disasters
- Special Forces operations

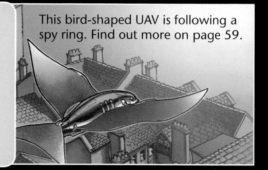

This bird-shaped UAV is following a spy ring. Find out more on page 59.

This UAV is searching a burning building to hunt for survivors. Find out more on pages 62-63.

Lending a hand

UAVs can be designed or adapted to cope with all sorts of conditions, and to carry equipment where it's needed.

- emergency rescue
- first aid

No limits

Drones offer new solutions to scientific projects.

- exploration
- conservation
- construction

This unmanned robot rover is exploring the surface of Mars. Find out more on pages 49-51.

Operating UAVs

Almost all UAVs have cameras and advanced sensors to examine their surroundings. Some can even send this information back to their operators in real time, using radio or satellite links.

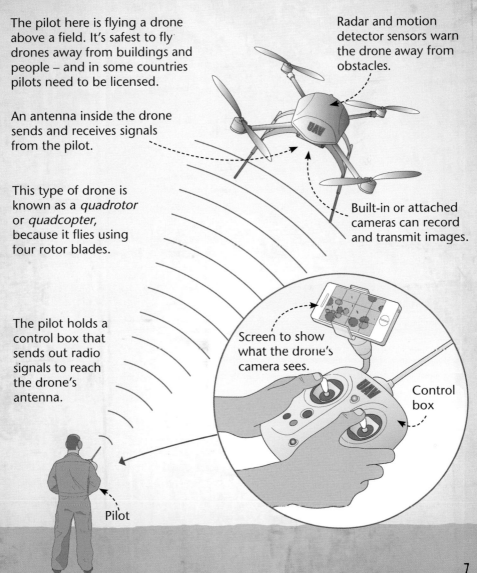

The pilot here is flying a drone above a field. It's safest to fly drones away from buildings and people – and in some countries pilots need to be licensed.

An antenna inside the drone sends and receives signals from the pilot.

This type of drone is known as a *quadrotor* or *quadcopter*, because it flies using four rotor blades.

The pilot holds a control box that sends out radio signals to reach the drone's antenna.

Radar and motion detector sensors warn the drone away from obstacles.

Built-in or attached cameras can record and transmit images.

Screen to show what the drone's camera sees.

Control box

Pilot

All shapes and sizes

With no need to provide space for human pilots or their safety equipment, drone designers are free to experiment with a great range of shapes and sizes.

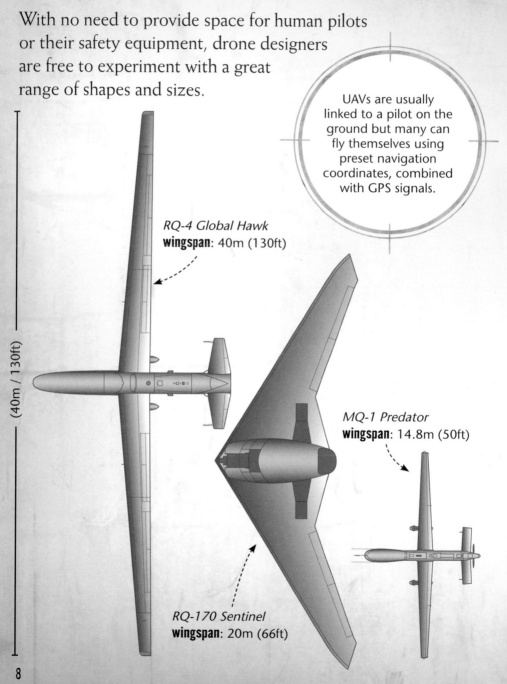

UAVs are usually linked to a pilot on the ground but many can fly themselves using preset navigation coordinates, combined with GPS signals.

RQ-4 Global Hawk
wingspan: 40m (130ft)

MQ-1 Predator
wingspan: 14.8m (50ft)

(40m / 130ft)

RQ-170 Sentinel
wingspan: 20m (66ft)

Better than human?

Some people argue that unmanned vehicles are the way of the future. Others prefer to keep humans in direct control...

Drone advantages	Drone disadvantages
• **Stamina** UAVs don't get sick, hungry or sleepy. With the help of in-flight refuelling, they can fly for days at a time. • **Agility** UAVs can make tight turns at very high speeds, well beyond human tolerances. • **Safety** A single UAV can carry out a range of tasks without having to worry about the safety of any on-board operator. • **Cost** UAVs, overall, are far cheaper than manned planes. Training remote pilots is cheaper and faster than training on-board pilots, too.	• **Impaired vision** Remote pilots can never get as good a look at the area around a drone as pilots inside the cockpit. • **Unreliable performance** Sensor technology is not as reliable as human reactions, so drone crashes are more common than manned plane crashes. • **Recklessness** Many critics believe drone pilots are more likely to make mistakes than fighter pilots, because their own safety is not at risk.

Although the smallest drones can fit into a matchbox, the remote control unit must be big enough for human hands to manipulate.

MQ-8 Fire Scout
length: 7m (23ft)

RQ-11B Raven
wingspan: 1.3m (4ft, 6in)

Parrot *AR.Drone 2.0*
length: 57cm (22in)

Person

Hubsan *Q4*

(4.5cm / 1.7in)

RQ-7 Shadow
wingspan: 4m (13ft)

senseFly *eBee*
wingspan: 96cm (3ft)

AscTec *Firefly*
length: 66cm (26in)

One of the longest-serving reconaissance drones is the *Global Hawk* UAV.

A *Global Hawk* can search and map out an area the size of Iceland in a single day.

Manufacturer

Name

Designation

Northrop Grumman *RQ-4 Global Hawk* UAV (US, 1998-present)

From nose to tail

- **Length:** 14.5m (47ft, 7in)
- **Wingspan:** 39.9m (130ft, 10in)
- **Endurance:** at least 24 hours
- **Max. speed:** 575km/h (357mph)
- **Main use:** reconaissance

Dates in active service with main operator

From wingtip to wingtip

How long the UAV can fly before needing fuel

Typical uses for this UAV

High fliers

High-altitude, long-range UAVs can fly at the far fringes of the Earth's atmosphere. Governments use them to photograph and monitor large areas of land and sea.

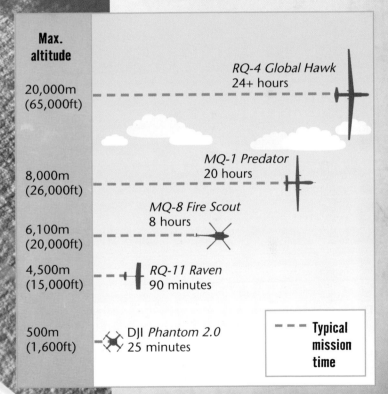

Max. altitude

20,000m (65,000ft) — RQ-4 Global Hawk, 24+ hours

8,000m (26,000ft) — MQ-1 Predator, 20 hours

6,100m (20,000ft) — MQ-8 Fire Scout, 8 hours

4,500m (15,000ft) — RQ-11 Raven, 90 minutes

500m (1,600ft) — DJI Phantom 2.0, 25 minutes

- - - - **Typical mission time**

The *Global Hawk* cruises for over 24 hours at a height of 18km (60,000ft). It can survey large areas of territory, searching for lost ships or charting desolate polar regions.

Inside a *Global Hawk*

UAVs share many similarities with planes, such as their basic shape – but the space inside can be used very differently. Here are some of the features found inside a *Global Hawk* surveillance drone.

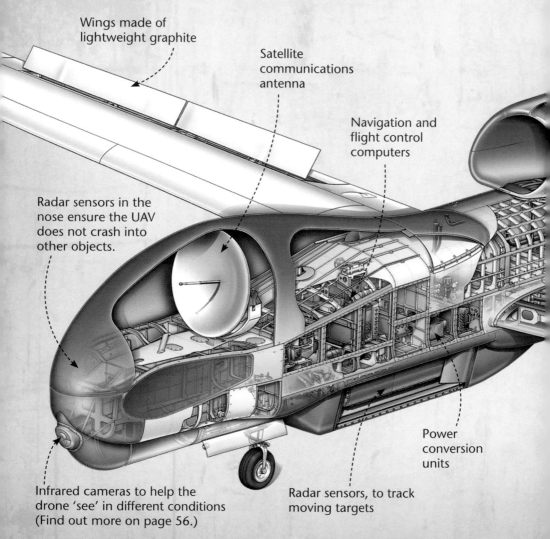

Wings made of lightweight graphite

Satellite communications antenna

Navigation and flight control computers

Radar sensors in the nose ensure the UAV does not crash into other objects.

Power conversion units

Infrared cameras to help the drone 'see' in different conditions (Find out more on page 56.)

Radar sensors, to track moving targets

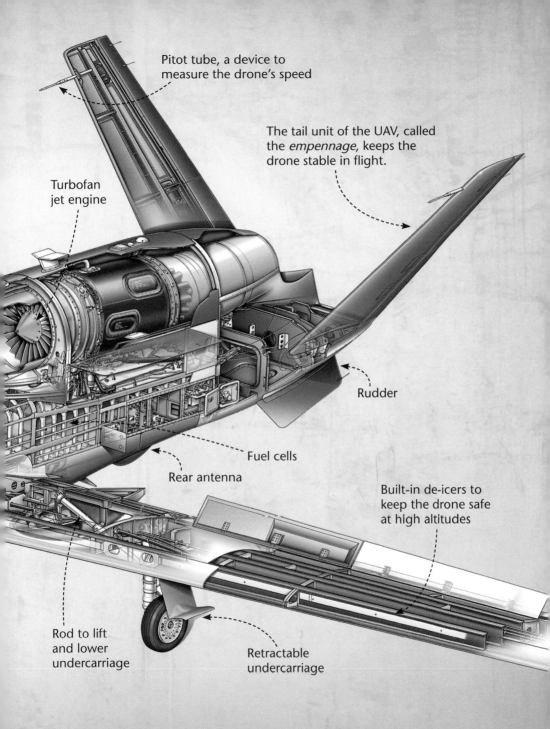

Pitot tube, a device to measure the drone's speed

The tail unit of the UAV, called the *empennage*, keeps the drone stable in flight.

Turbofan jet engine

Rudder

Fuel cells

Rear antenna

Built-in de-icers to keep the drone safe at high altitudes

Rod to lift and lower undercarriage

Retractable undercarriage

Remote control

Pilots operate long-range UAVs from a *ground control station*, or *GCS*. These can be located miles away from the flying zone.

Meet the crew

Most UCAVs require two operators. A *pilot* handles the flying. A *sensor operator*, or *copilot*, monitors the cameras, guidance systems and communications.

Mobile command

Many UAV operations are run by a GCS within a few miles of the target. A mobile GCS is a steel cabin small enough to be carried by a truck, or even on a plane, so it can be shipped all around the world.

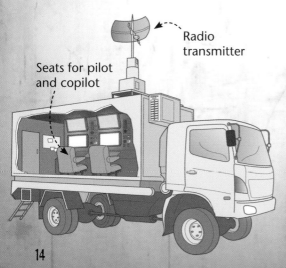

Radio transmitter

Seats for pilot and copilot

Map displaying roads on the ground below the drone.

Screen relaying real-time images from the UAV's nose cameras

Joystick to control drone's wings and propellers

Early experiments

Drones can strike at an enemy without risking the lives of soldiers or a crew. Military leaders have encouraged inventors to develop these battle-winning weapons for hundreds of years.

Fire at sea

Some of the very oldest unmanned vehicles were *fireships*, used in sea battles. Crews would set fire to an abandoned ship, then release it to be pushed along by the wind towards an enemy target.

Dutch captain Jan van Brankel used fireships to burn and sink the English warship *Royal James* during the Battle of Solebay in 1672.

Basket bombs

In 1849 the Austrian army pioneered the first UAVs – balloons loaded with bombs sent to destroy the city of Venice.

On board ships, soldiers attached bombs and timers to more than 100 balloons. With the wind on their side, they released the balloons.

The timers and bombs worked well enough, but the balloons were at the mercy of changing winds.

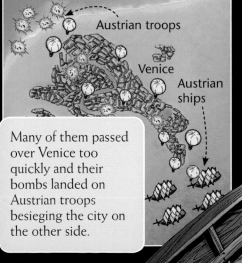

Austrian troops

Venice

Austrian ships

Many of them passed over Venice too quickly and their bombs landed on Austrian troops besieging the city on the other side.

When the timers ran down, each bomb detached from its balloon, fell to the ground...

...and exploded.

And some balloons blew back over their own launch ships before releasing their deadly cargo.

Flying torpedoes

After the breakthrough in powered flight of the early 1900s, military engineers started to experiment with flying bombs. The US Army asked inventor Charles Kettering to build one of the very first drone missiles, known as the *Bug*.

Flying the *Bug*

The *Bug* was launched from a wooden frame called a *dolly*, that rode along rails.

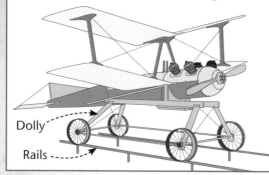

Dolly

Rails

- **Length:** 7m (23ft, 11in)
- **Wingspan:** 9m (29ft, 4in)
- **Range:** 120km (75 miles)
- **Speed:** 175km/h (109mph)
- **Main use:** destroying distant ground targets

The *Bug* was still being tested when the First World War ended in 1918. It was never used in actual combat.

1 **Launch** The *Bug*'s propeller pulled it along the rails. It lifted away from the dolly and into the sky.

2 **In flight** Equipment such as *gyroscopes*, an *altimeter* and a *speed sensor* kept the *Bug* level and on course.

3 **Strike** After a pre-set number of turns, the engine cut out and the wings fell away.

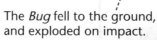

2

3

1

The *Bug* fell to the ground, and exploded on impact.

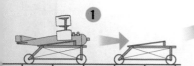

Remote control

In the 1930s, British inventors replaced pilots in the cockpit with radio flying controls. The British Royal Navy used these early 'drones' as moving targets for training. As radio controls improved, engineers made plans to send them into battle.

British Prime Minister Winston Churchill observes the launch of a *Queen Bee* UAV, used as a target for warship gunners and fighter pilots during training.

DH.82B *Queen Bee* UAV
(UK, 1941–1946)

- **Length:** 7m (23ft, 11in)
- **Wingspan:** 9m (29ft, 4in)
- **Endurance:** around 4 hours
- **Speed:** 175km/h (109mph)
- **Main use:** target practice for Navy gunners

The *Queen Bee* was adapted from a *Tiger Moth* training plane, fitted with radio controls in the cockpit.

The body, or *fuselage*, was made of wood to save on costs.

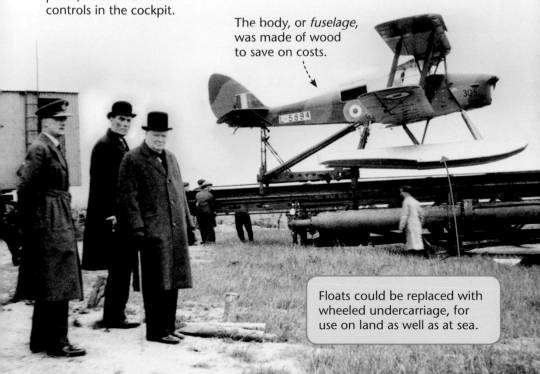

Floats could be replaced with wheeled undercarriage, for use on land as well as at sea.

Staying on target

After takeoff, most flying machines rely on sensors, computers and other tools to keep them level and on course. At the heart of these controls is a simple spinning device, called a *gyroscope*.

Gyroscopes, gimbals and drones

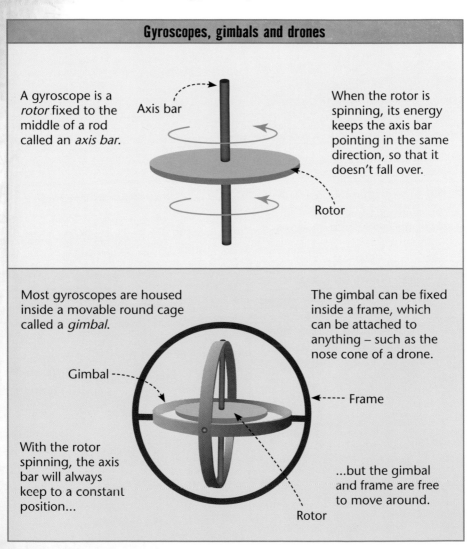

A gyroscope is a *rotor* fixed to the middle of a rod called an *axis bar*.

Axis bar

When the rotor is spinning, its energy keeps the axis bar pointing in the same direction, so that it doesn't fall over.

Rotor

Most gyroscopes are housed inside a movable round cage called a *gimbal*.

Gimbal

With the rotor spinning, the axis bar will always keep to a constant position...

The gimbal can be fixed inside a frame, which can be attached to anything – such as the nose cone of a drone.

Frame

...but the gimbal and frame are free to move around.

Rotor

Using gyroscopes to navigate

1 Even though the gimbal tilts up or down with the movements of a drone in flight...

...the axis bar in the gyroscope doesn't change position.

2 A computer can measure the exact amount that the drone moves compared to the axis bar.

3 The same computer then adjusts the flight of the drone, to keep it on course.

Modern UAVs use electronic gyroscope chips that can measure and adjust tiny movements of a drone with great accuracy.

V-2 rockets were some of the first successful drones. Find out more on page 22.

Gyroscopes in the nose cone kept a *V-2* on target.

A longer reach

The development of jets and rocket engines during the Second World War (1939-45) allowed unmanned guided bombs and missiles to fly the first long-range UAV missions.

V-1 bombs were pointed in the right direction on launch. An in-built compass kept each bomb on course, while a pendulum sensor stopped it from pitching up or down too far.

V-1 Maikäfer/Buzz bomb flying bomb
(Germany, 1944–1945)

- **Length:** 8.3m (27ft, 2in)
- **Max. range:** 250km (160 miles)
- **Top speed:** 640km/h (400mph)
- **Weapon carried:** 850kg (1,870lbs) explosive

V-2 rocket bomb
(Germany, 1944–1952)

- **Length:** 14m (45ft, 11in)
- **Max. range:** 320km (200 miles)
- **Top speed:** 5,760km/h (3,580mph)
- **Weapon carried:** 1,000kg (2,200lbs) explosive

V-2s used rocket engines to power them to the edge of the Earth's atmosphere before dropping to the ground.

Vanes ----

Metal flaps around the rocket exhaust, known as *vanes*, made adjustments to the bomb's course.

SM-62 *Snark* cruise missile
(USA, 1959–1961)

- **Length:** 20.5m (67ft, 2in)
- **Max. range:** 250km (160 miles)
- **Top speed:** 10,200km/h (6,300mph)
- **Weapon carried:** nuclear warhead

Missiles were often known as *fire-and-forget* weapons, as ground crews had little control over them after launch.

The *Snark* used celestial navigation – following the stars. But this system was rarely accurate.

Tomahawk cruise missile
(USA, 1983–present)

- **Length:** 5.5m (18ft, 4in)
- **Max. range:** 2,500km (1,550 miles)
- **Top speed:** 890km/h (550mph)
- **Weapon carried:** 450kg (1,000lbs) explosive warhead

Tomahawk uses radar to study the terrain it flies over. It compares this with maps stored on its computers and adjusts its direction to stay on course.

Storm Shadow cruise missile
(France/Italy/UK, 2002–present)

- **Length:** 5.1m (16ft, 6in)
- **Max. range:** 250km (160 miles)
- **Top speed:** 1,000km/h (620mph)
- **Weapon carried:** 450kg (1,000lbs) explosive or metal-piercing warhead

Storm Shadow missiles use radar combined with live input from satellites, providing information about the terrain below.

Fold-out wings

Fighting fire with fire

SITUATION: In 1944, the German army launched a secret drone weapon to attack their enemies in London – the *V-1* flying bomb.

Each *V-1* bomb was accurate enough to hit a specific city and cause great damage at no risk to German lives.

British and US generals decided to build their own drones to smash the *V-1* bases in northern France.

In an ultra-secret mission codenamed *Aphrodite*, British and American air crews took old *B-17* bomber planes and stuffed them with high explosives and radio controls.

Pilots sitting inside the *Aphrodite* drones guided them into the air. A manned mothership, usually another *B-17*, flew close behind.

Manned mothership

Unmanned drone

Once on course, the pilot activated the radio controls in his *Aphrodite* drone, then bailed out, using a parachute.

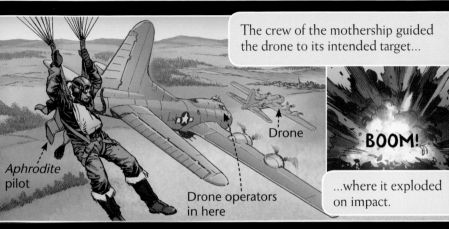

The crew of the mothership guided the drone to its intended target...

Aphrodite pilot

Drone

Drone operators in here

BOOM!

...where it exploded on impact.

At least twenty *Aphrodite* drones flew into battle, but only one was successfully activated. Even then, it landed short of its target.

The radio control system was very unreliable, and most planes landed much too early, or fell into the sea.

The *V-1* and, later, *V-2* drone attacks rained havoc over Britain until the RAF destroyed their bases in 1945.

Eyes in the sky

Carrying the latest camera technology, drones offer their pilots a bird's-eye view of any battlefield.

Infantry teams can transport medium-sized, short-range UAVs very close to enemy territory, and deploy them within minutes.

Rheinmetall *KZO* UAV	
(Germany, 2005–present)	

- **Length:** 2.3m (7ft, 6in)
- **Wingspan:** 3.4m (11ft)
- **Range:** at least 100km (62 miles)
- **Speed:** 220km/h (135mph)
- **Main use:** surveillance

A clear signal

Short-range UAVs are controlled via signals from a GCS mast. The GCS keeps in constant radio contact with the drone – as long as it avoids flying behind obstacles such as hills or tall buildings.

This radio mast maintains a short-range link with the drone. A separate truck houses the pilots, and carries a more powerful mast.

This *KZO* is launching from a truck using rocket boosters.

The *KZO* has no undercarriage or skids to make a landing. Instead, it deploys a parachute and drops slowly to the ground.

KZO surveillance drones have flown more than 2,000 missions since they were first used in 2009, in Afghanistan.

Angle of drone's nose cone

Weapons targeting laser

Exact location of the UAV

Targeting tool

Basic flight data

ACFT
N 36°38'43"
W115°39'43"
7,474 HAT

Laser ARMED

-177

1
EA
/117
3
C

-42

LTHC

N 36°40'05"
W115°39'28"
BRG 8
RNG 3,431H
RNG 1.85NH
THD 38H
ELV 2966F

Double act drones

On some missions, pilots need to take a UAV over obstacles that block the signal from their GCS. One solution is to use a *relay* drone, to extend the control signal.

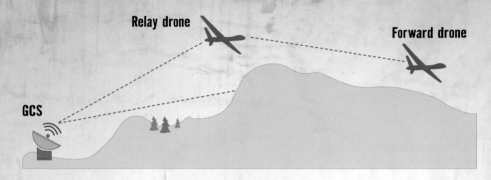

Relay drone

Forward drone

GCS

All around the world

Drones can fly further, even across continents, by relaying their control signal via satellites that manage *GPS* – the *Global Positioning System*.

A ring of satellites in space means that a UAV can be located by up to three satellites at all times.

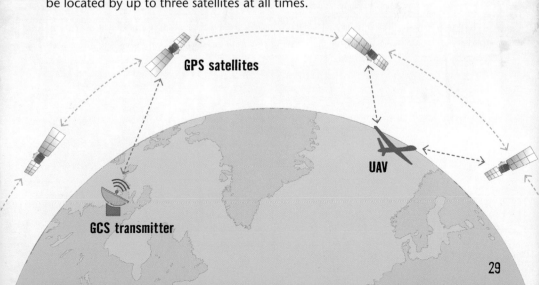

GPS satellites

UAV

GCS transmitter

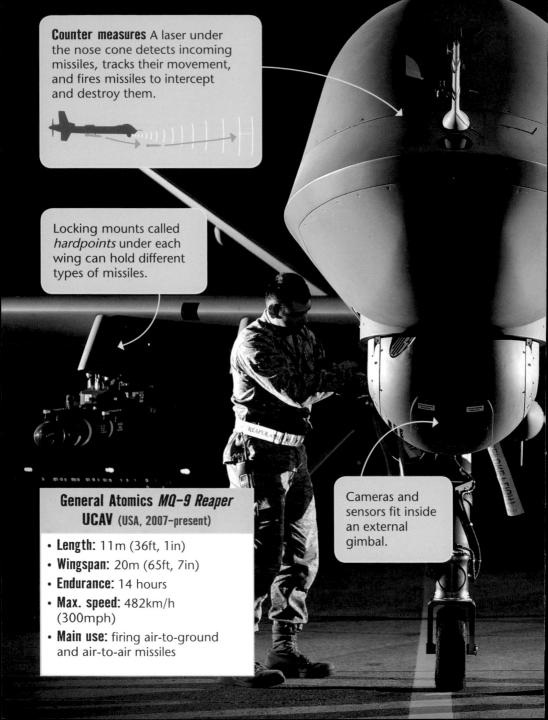

Counter measures A laser under the nose cone detects incoming missiles, tracks their movement, and fires missiles to intercept and destroy them.

Locking mounts called *hardpoints* under each wing can hold different types of missiles.

General Atomics *MQ-9 Reaper* UCAV (USA, 2007–present)

- **Length:** 11m (36ft, 1in)
- **Wingspan:** 20m (65ft, 7in)
- **Endurance:** 14 hours
- **Max. speed:** 482km/h (300mph)
- **Main use:** firing air-to-ground and air-to-air missiles

Cameras and sensors fit inside an external gimbal.

Into battle

Drones don't always take a back seat in a firefight. Combat drones, or *Unmanned Combat Aerial Vehicles* (UCAVs), such as this *MQ-9 Reaper*, carry missiles and other deadly weapons.

Hellfire missiles Once launched, each missile activates its own jet engine. Cameras and laser-guiding sensors in the drone's nose cone allow the pilot to guide the missile.

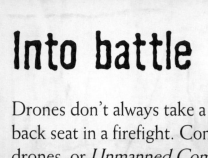

Warbirds

A fleet of state-of-the-art UCAVs gives today's global superpowers huge military advantages on any battlefield.

General Atomics *Avenger* UCAV
(USA, 2009–present)

- **Length:** 13m (44ft)
- **Wingspan:** 20m (66ft)
- **Endurance:** 18 hours
- **Max. speed:** 740km/h (460mph)
- **Main use:** search and destroy

The Avenger can carry internal weapons as well as hardpoint-mounted missiles.

The wings and fuselage of combat drones are often painted in drab, light hues, to disguise them from ground spotters.

Northrop Grumman *MQ-8C Fire Scout* UAS
(USA, 2014 – present day)

- **Length:** 12.6m (41ft, 3in)
- **Endurance:** 12 hours
- **Max. speed:** 250km/h (155mph)
- **Main uses:** enhanced situational awareness

The original *MQ-8A Fire Scouts* were used only for real-time mission monitoring. Models 8B and 8C are able to carry weapons.

The distinctive design of the *X-47B* helps mask it from radar detection.

Northrop Grumman *X-47B* UCAS
(USA, 2011–present day)

- **Length:** 11.6m (38ft, 1in)
- **Wingspan:** 18.9m (62ft, 1in)
- **Range:** at least 3,900km (2,400 miles)
- **Speed:** high subsonic
- **Main use:** demonstration model for the U.S. Navy

The wingtips can fold up so lots of *X-47*s can fit snugly inside aircraft carrier hangar bays.

It carries missiles inside its fuselage, to keep its stealth design.

BAE Systems *Taranis* UCAV
(UK, still in development)

- **Length:** 12.4m (40ft, 9in)
- **Wingspan:** 10m (32ft, 10in)
- **Endurance:** at least 24 hours
- **Speed:** high subsonic
- **Main use:** stealth bomber

The *Taranis* is being designed to fly under its own control for some missions, with no need for a human pilot on the ground.

33

A day in the life

Being a drone pilot is not so very different from having an office job. Pilots don't have to live on a military base, and can have a normal home life.

For many drone pilots, a daily shift of 8-12 hours begins with a commute to work...

07:00 local time

...followed by an identity check.

After changing into flight uniform, the pilot and his operator enter the Ground Control Station to take over the controls of a *Reaper* UCAV...

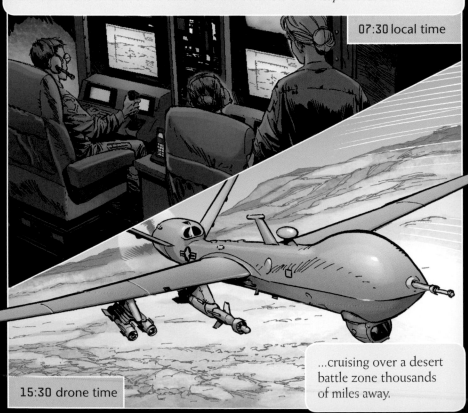

07:30 local time

15:30 drone time

...cruising over a desert battle zone thousands of miles away.

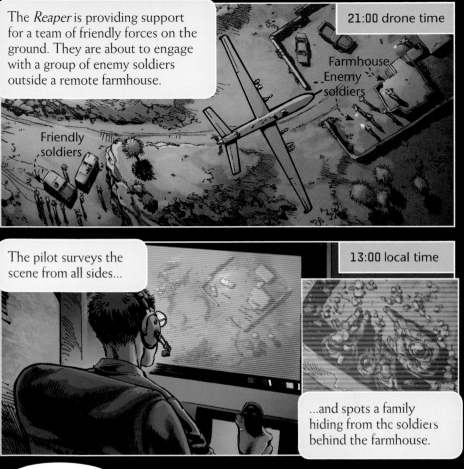

The *Reaper* is providing support for a team of friendly forces on the ground. They are about to engage with a group of enemy soldiers outside a remote farmhouse.

21:00 drone time

Farmhouse
Enemy soldiers

Friendly soldiers

The pilot surveys the scene from all sides...

13:00 local time

...and spots a family hiding from the soldiers behind the farmhouse.

Call off the attack! Civilians on the ground.

Roger that, Reaper team.

18:00 local time

Though safe from harm, drone pilots may suffer aftershocks of combat stress. It can be hard adjusting to home life just moments after flying a combat mission.

On solid ground

Engineers are testing a range of drone
land vehicles to move heavy loads
and take on dangerous jobs.

QinetiQ *Dragon Runner 20* SUGV
(UK/USA, in development)

- **Length:** 41cm (16in)
- **Endurance:** up to 4 hours
- **Max. speed:** 6.5km/h
  (4mph)
- **Main uses:** urban combat
  surveillance; finding explosives

It has four cameras,
including night vision to
help it work in darkness.

Soldiers can carry a *Dragon
Runner* in a backpack, and
throw it over a wall to launch
it into a combat zone.

Its tracks can
climb stairs.

Driverless drones

Unmanned Ground Vehicles, or *UGVs*, can be remotely driven or even work autonomously – without needing a human driver. It's not always possible to tell whether a large UGV has a driver inside or not.

G–NIUS *Guardium* UGV
(Israel, 2009–present)

- **Length:** 2.95m (9ft, 8in)
- **Endurance:** several days
- **Max. speed:** 80km/h (50mph)
- **Main use:** surveillance

Remote drivers can communicate directly with people near the *Guardium* through a set of loudspeakers and microphones.

Antenna array to send and receive information

Sensor array includes night vision capabilities

Cameras provide 360° views around the drone.

The *Guardium* can activate an autonomous driving mode to tackle routine border patrols.

Scouting ahead

Small UAVs are portable and quick to assemble and launch. Field teams can use them to gather and share battlefield information.

Camera and sensor array

Puma small UAV

Propeller makes almost no sound.

Hand-launch is completely silent.

This training exercise shows US and Philippino forces working together.

The *Puma* can land on water. Once retrieved by its operator, it is ready for another mission.

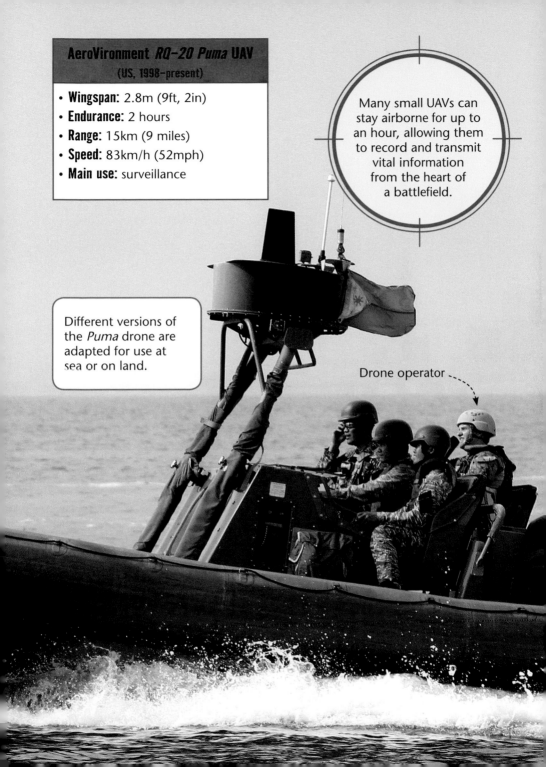

AeroVironment *RQ-20 Puma* UAV
(US, 1998-present)

- **Wingspan:** 2.8m (9ft, 2in)
- **Endurance:** 2 hours
- **Range:** 15km (9 miles)
- **Speed:** 83km/h (52mph)
- **Main use:** surveillance

Many small UAVs can stay airborne for up to an hour, allowing them to record and transmit vital information from the heart of a battlefield.

Different versions of the *Puma* drone are adapted for use at sea or on land.

Drone operator

Thrown into action

Some UGVs are so small that soldiers can simply throw them over a wall or into a building. Like short-range drones, these *throwable robots* can carry cameras, sensors and even weapons.

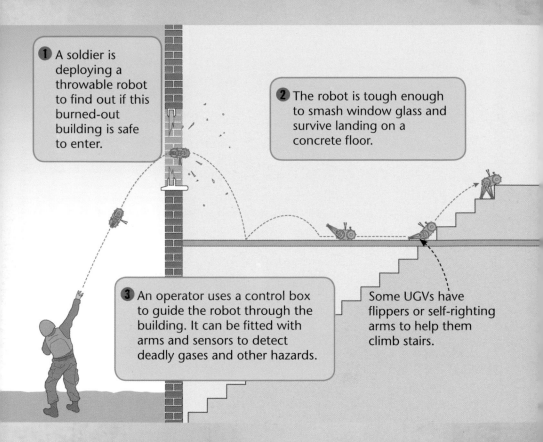

1 A soldier is deploying a throwable robot to find out if this burned-out building is safe to enter.

2 The robot is tough enough to smash window glass and survive landing on a concrete floor.

3 An operator uses a control box to guide the robot through the building. It can be fitted with arms and sensors to detect deadly gases and other hazards.

Some UGVs have flippers or self-righting arms to help them climb stairs.

Seeing around corners

UGVs and throwables give soldiers and emergency services real-time pictures of any threats and action happening around them. This vital information is known as *situational awareness*.

Air attack

SITUATION: A police special forces team has chased a gang of armed bank robbers from a crime scene to their hideout.

Safe on the roof, the gang open fire, preventing the team from coming closer.

Behind the police van, a pilot launches a drone from a tube. He guides it high over the rooftop.

Wings unfold in flight.

I have them in my sights. Ready to deploy grenade.

The gang doesn't hear the silent drone approaching.

By the time they spot the drone and fire on it, the pilot has already armed its weapon system.

A burst of bright light stuns the gang. The police rush in to make arrests in safety.

The wings fold in, and a flash grenade explodes.

Working the land

It can take weeks to master flying a drone, but the end results can save months of time and effort. People around the world are building and using drones to help with a range of tasks on farms, land and construction sites.

Farmers use UAVs to give them an overhead view of their fields. Heat sensors on the drone detect any areas in the crop where plants might be suffering from disease or pests.

Drone operator

Farmers can even use drone sensors to measure the exact height of plants in their crop, to help them plan for the harvest.

This UAV is fitted with a sprayer to treat the crop with nutrients and protect it from harmful insects.

Getting the job done

Mapping the land

UAVs quickly photograph and measure the physical features on the ground, helping surveyors and construction teams.

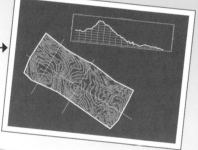

Brick by brick

Drones are learning to tackle repetitive tasks, such as stacking crates.

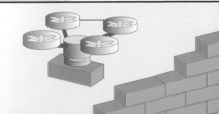

Compared to UAVs, camera teams on the ground find it hard to keep up with skiers as they race down slopes and perform dramatic jumps.

Getting the shot

Sporting clubs and officials can send drones to film events. UAVs are cheaper and safer to use around athletes than helicopters, and can fly within a few feet of the action.

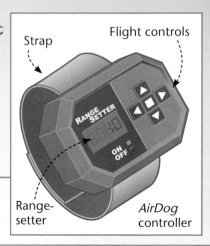

This drone camera is following competitors during the 2012 Alpine skiing World Cup, held in Switzerland.

The Olympic Winter Games held at Sochi, Russia, in 2014, was one of the first major sporting events to see use of drone cameras across multiple events.

Drone on a leash

Sports competitors can control their own personal camera drones, such as the *AirDog* or the *Nixie*, using a wrist-mounted controller.

The controller sets a range, which tethers the drone using a virtual leash created by radio waves.

Strap

Flight controls

RANGE SETTER

ON
OFF

The drone can now follow and film all the action from above.

Range-setter

AirDog controller

Deep blue drones

Marine drones explore and patrol the world's oceans. Many follow a pre-set course, using sensors to navigate without any human operator. These *Autonomous Underwater Vehicles*, or *AUVs*, can venture out on quick surveys or year-long missions.

Seafox AUV
(USA, 2009–present)

- **Length:** 1.3m (4ft, 2in)
- **Max. depth:** 300m (980ft)
- **Endurance:** 1 hour
- **Max. speed:** 11km/h (7mph)
- **Main use:** patrolling waters and finding hidden dangers

The *Seafox*, or similar AUVs, are carried by many warships.

It can set explosive charges to destroy underwater mines or cut snagging cables.

RU–27 Scarlet Knight AUV
(USA, 2009–present)

Scarlet Knight was the first AUV to cross the Atlantic Ocean.

- **Length:** 2.5m (8ft)
- **Max. depth:** 200m (66ft)
- **Endurance:** up to 1 year
- **Speed:** 7km/h (4mph)
- **Main use:** exploration, data gathering

It drifts on currents, diving and ascending to record water temperature and other information.

ACTUVs have a sleek hull design that hides them from warship sensors.

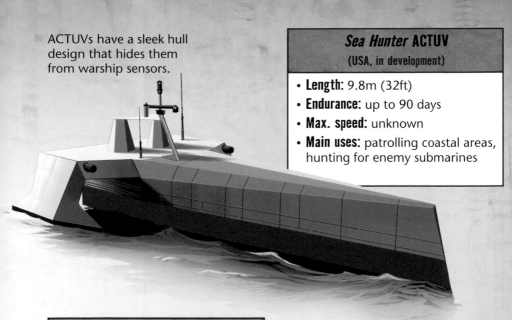

Sea Hunter ACTUV
(USA, in development)

- **Length:** 9.8m (32ft)
- **Endurance:** up to 90 days
- **Max. speed:** unknown
- **Main uses:** patrolling coastal areas, hunting for enemy submarines

REMUS 100 AUV
(USA, in development)

- **Length:** 10.6m (34ft, 8in)
- **Endurance:** 14 hours
- **Max. speed:** 9km/h (6mph)
- **Main uses:** data gathering; deep sea search and rescue

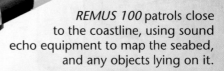

REMUS 100 patrols close to the coastline, using sound echo equipment to map the seabed, and any objects lying on it.

Many AUVs struggle in choppy waters. The *BioSwimmer* design copies the body shape of a tuna fish, making it nimble in waves or below the surface.

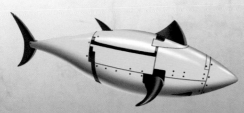

BioSwimmer AUV
(USA, in development)

- **Length:** 2.9m (ft, in)
- **Endurance:** up to 22 hours
- **Max. speed:** 19km/h (12mph)
- **Main use:** exploring hard-to-reach areas, such as shipwrecks

Into space

Vast, dangerous and uncharted, deep space is the toughest environment for any pilot or machine. Drones and remote-control robots have been vital tools for the world's space agencies since the 1960s.

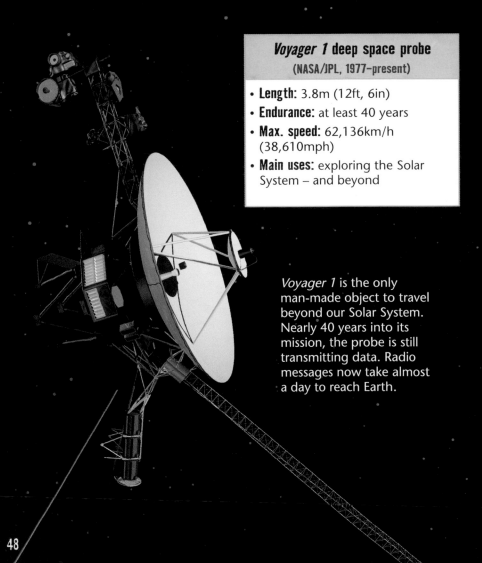

Voyager 1 deep space probe
(NASA/JPL, 1977–present)

- **Length:** 3.8m (12ft, 6in)
- **Endurance:** at least 40 years
- **Max. speed:** 62,136km/h (38,610mph)
- **Main uses:** exploring the Solar System – and beyond

Voyager 1 is the only man-made object to travel beyond our Solar System. Nearly 40 years into its mission, the probe is still transmitting data. Radio messages now take almost a day to reach Earth.

Progress robot spacecraft

(USSR/Russia, 1978–present)

- **Length:** 7.2m (23ft, 8in)
- **Endurance:** up to 6 months
- **Orbital speed:** 28,044km/h (17,426mph)
- **Main uses:** carrying cargo

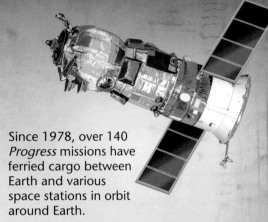

Since 1978, over 140 *Progress* missions have ferried cargo between Earth and various space stations in orbit around Earth.

Curiosity rover

(NASA, 2012–present day)

- **Length:** 2.9m (9ft, 6in)
- **Endurance:** at least 2 years
- **Max. speed:** 0.9km/h (0.5mph)
- **Main uses:** exploration and sample collecting

The most distant robot in use today is on Mars, gathering information that could be useful for a manned mission to that planet. Find out more on page 50.

X–37 spaceplane

(NASA/USAF, 2010–present)

- **Length:** 8.9m (29ft, 3in)
- **Endurance:** up to 270 days
- **Orbital speed:** 28,044km/h (17,426mph)
- **Main use:** transporting goods between Earth and spacecraft in orbit around Earth

Spaceplanes are designed to work in outer space and in Earth's atmosphere, so that they can land like a plane and be re-used later.

Eyes on Mars

Dateline: 26 November 2011

Situation: An *Atlas V* rocket was the first step in an explorer drone's journey to Mars, the Red Planet.

Space cruiser in here

Rocket boosters

The rocket blasted free of Earth's atmosphere before releasing a cruiser module that held the drone.

Moving at over 93,000km/h (58,000mph), the cruiser set out on its nine-month flight to Mars.

Curiosity is loaded with sensors to help it explore and study Mars.

The drone, known as the *Curiosity* rover, was in here.

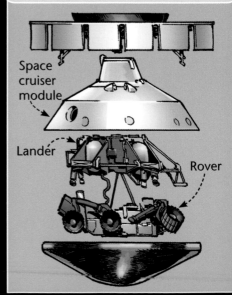

Space cruiser module

Lander

Rover

After entering Mars' atmosphere, the rover and its landing vehicle broke free from the cruiser.

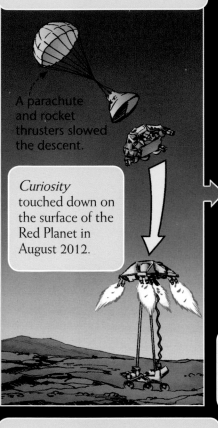

A parachute and rocket thrusters slowed the descent.

Curiosity touched down on the surface of the Red Planet in August 2012.

Since 2012, a transmitter on Earth has beamed signals across space to a set of satellites in orbit around Mars.

At certain times of day, *Curiosity* can beam back images and data. It takes up to 20 minutes for the data to cross space and arrive on Earth.

Operators on Earth program a work schedule for *Curiosity* every day.

Curiosity has already found signs of water on Mars. It's unlikely, but one day it may even find signs of life...

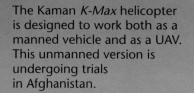

The Kaman *K-Max* helicopter is designed to work both as a manned vehicle and as a UAV. This unmanned version is undergoing trials in Afghanistan.

Danger watch

Drones help emergency teams reach accident and disaster sites quickly. They can also deliver medical supplies or carry water to battle raging fires.

Using a rope, the UAV can lift cargo weighing up to 3,000kg (6,600lbs)

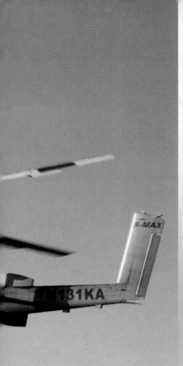

Weather combat

Drones fly at high altitudes to track storms and developing weather systems. They carry the latest meteorological sensors and powerful cameras.

This illustration shows a *Global Hawk* drone flying above a hurricane. Experts at the controls can use data from the drone's sensors to predict the course of the storm.

Where drones dare

Pilots use cameras on their drone to guide it around obstacles, through narrow gaps and even into places that would be deadly for any human pilot to enter.

This drone pilot is flying a DJI *Phantom 2* quadcopter drone over the mouth of the Bardarbunga Volcano, in Iceland, during an eruption in 2014.

Drone controller

This screen shows the drone's FPV.

A second drone was able to film the lead drone as it flew over the smoking crater. The lead drone was destroyed by the ferocious heat.

To the ends of the Earth	
Environment	**How drones have been used**
Into a storm	September 2014: US weather researchers flew a *Coyote* drone into the eye of Hurricane Edouard as it raged over the North Atlantic.
Under the ice	December 2014: Researchers in Antarctica began using undersea drones to investigate micro-organisms that live on the underside of the polar ice.
Through deep caves	March 2015: Photographer Ryan Deboodt explored the world's largest cave, Hang Son Doong in Vietnam, using a specialized UAV.

All-seeing eyes

Miles above the ground, a drone needs to keep its cameras and other optical sensors steady and locked on target. Like a gyroscope, these are fixed inside a rotating gimbal, allowing them to turn and focus while the drone changes direction in the sky.

Tip of the drone's nose cone

Laser rangefinder

Gimbal holding cameras and sensors

Cooling fan

What the sensors see

1 SAR sensor
A type of radar that can build up a map of the terrain and buildings below, even in thick smoke or total darkness.

2 Two video cameras
One is used by the pilot, the other carries out a wide-sweeping ground surveillance.

3 Infrared camera
This detects heat differences between objects, allowing the pilot to track people, gunfire and vehicle engines, even in darkness.

City watch

A single drone fitted with a new camera system, known as *ARGUS-IS,* can keep watch over an area the size of a small city. The system can follow and record individual cars and pedestrians, even without a pilot.

How *Argus-IS* works

The camera system is made up of hundreds of separate image processors, all pointed in slightly different directions. Each one records the images it sees.

A computer in the drone's control station joins all the images together to make a single patchwork image.

An *ARGUS-IS* operator can zoom in on each individual square, to see the view through a single image processor.

The view from each image processor is detailed enough to pick out individual cars and pedestrians.

The long arm of the law

Police teams are testing small UAVs to see if they can replace expensive manned helicopters in fighting crime, keeping traffic moving and patrolling border crossings.

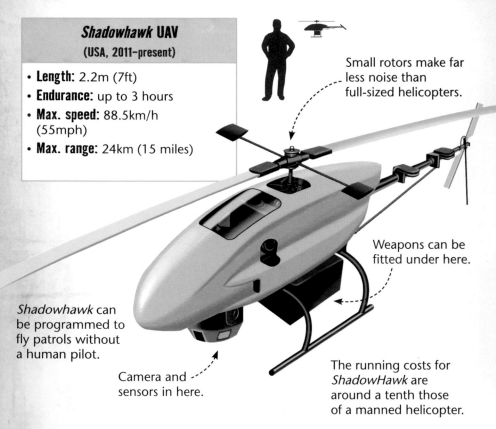

Shadowhawk UAV
(USA, 2011–present)

- **Length:** 2.2m (7ft)
- **Endurance:** up to 3 hours
- **Max. speed:** 88.5km/h (55mph)
- **Max. range:** 24km (15 miles)

Small rotors make far less noise than full-sized helicopters.

Weapons can be fitted under here.

Shadowhawk can be programmed to fly patrols without a human pilot.

Camera and sensors in here.

The running costs for *ShadowHawk* are around a tenth those of a manned helicopter.

Shadowhawk in action

If it passes trials, *Shadowhawk* could be used:
- to scout and report on road repair works and traffic jams
- to provide live pictures of police Special Weapons and Tactics, or SWAT operations, including hostage rescues
- to sweep wilderness areas for missing persons
- to guard border crossings, by photographing and identifying smugglers

Spies in the sky

Spy agencies are developing drones disguised as birds that can follow and film suspects without attracting attention.

This spy has tailed a target to a building. From a safe distance, she launches a bird drone.

In flight, the drone flaps its wings.

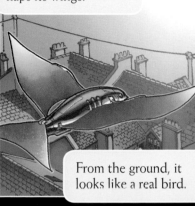

From the ground, it looks like a real bird.

The drone lands on a power line. It can recharge its batteries using solar panels on its back, or by wirelessly connecting to a transformer.

Cameras and microphones in the 'head'

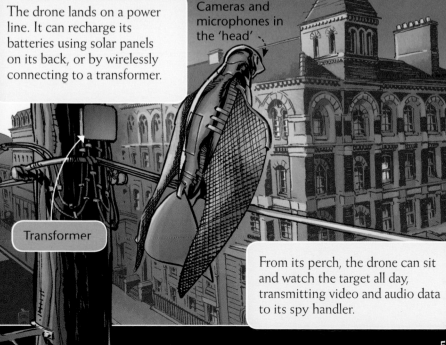

Transformer

From its perch, the drone can sit and watch the target all day, transmitting video and audio data to its spy handler.

Quadrotor drones and radio-controlled helicopters have similar features and capabilities, but quadrotors use fewer complex parts and are cheaper to build.

The rotors work in pairs. Two spin in one direction, the other two spin in the opposite direction. This keeps the drone steady.

Hover birds

Drones known as *quadrotors* have four separate rotors that let them fly, hover in place and even perform complex aerial stunts. Like helicopters, they can take off and land by going straight up or down.

This is a custom-built nano-quadrotor drone, adapted from a *Crazyflie 2.0*, used as part of a team of drones that can form structures.

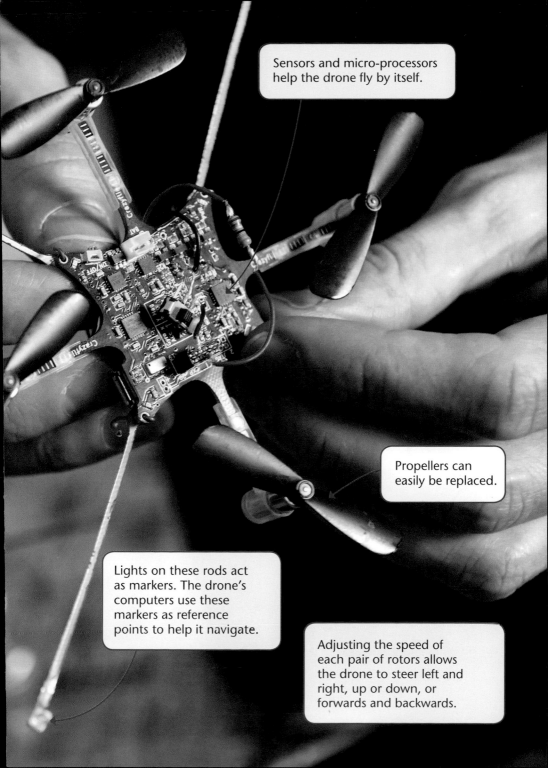

Fire rescue

SITUATION: A towering inner city office building is on fire. While firefighters attack the flames, one crew member deploys a drone.

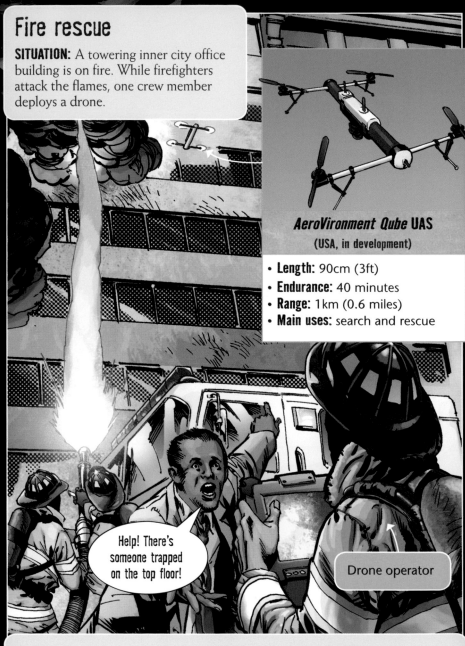

AeroVironment Qube UAS
(USA, in development)

- **Length:** 90cm (3ft)
- **Endurance:** 40 minutes
- **Range:** 1km (0.6 miles)
- **Main uses:** search and rescue

Help! There's someone trapped on the top floor!

Drone operator

Emergency services around the world are testing out many different drones, including the *Qube*. These drones provide a close-up view of the fire from any angle, and are far cheaper to operate than manned helicopters.

With the help of heat sensors and cameras, the pilot guides the drone in through an open window.

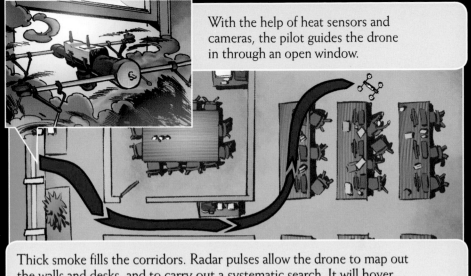

Thick smoke fills the corridors. Radar pulses allow the drone to map out the walls and desks, and to carry out a systematic search. It will hover beside any survivors it finds.

The survivor speaks to the operator through a two-way radio on the drone.

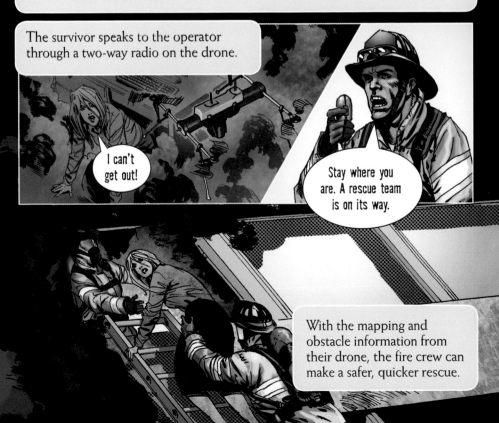

I can't get out!

Stay where you are. A rescue team is on its way.

With the mapping and obstacle information from their drone, the fire crew can make a safer, quicker rescue.

Nanodrones

Many drones are small enough to fit inside your pocket, but they still have some amazing abilities.

NUAV stands for *Nano Unmanned Air Vehicle* – a designation used for very small drones.

PD-PRS *Black Hornet 2* NUAV

(Norway, 2012–present)

- **Length:** 16cm (6.25in)
- **Endurance:** 25 minutes
- **Max. speed:** 18km/h (11mph)
- **Main use:** surveillance

The electric motors are almost silent, making the *Black Hornet* ideal for stealth operations.

This *Black Hornet* is flying into a fire. The operators can use its cameras and sensors to see through the blaze.

The British Army has already deployed hundreds of *Black Hornets* to help with operations in Afghanistan.

The *Hummingbird* drone is smaller and lighter than the largest real-life hummingbirds.

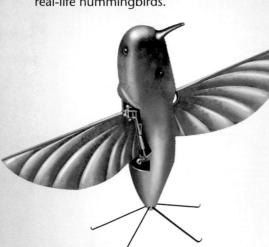

Hummingbird compared to an adult.

Hubsan *Q4/A* nano quadrotor
(China, 2013–present)

- **Length:** 4.5cm (1.8in)
- **Endurance:** up to 8 minutes
- **Max. speed:** 40km/h (25mph)
- **Main use:** leisure

The *Q4* is smaller than your palm, but it can hover, flip and perform other flying stunts. LED lights show the pilot which way the drone is facing.

Red lights on the back rotors

Doctors have already built pea-sized drone capsules. These contain cameras that patients can swallow to photograph their digestive system.

Blue lights on the front

This picture shows the *Q4* at actual size.

Problem solving

Designers can add parts, sensors and other equipment to the frame of a UAV to help it perform different tasks. For specific jobs, a designer might come up with an entirely new shape.

Flying doctor

Still being tested, the *ambulance drone* transports life-saving medical equipment to heart attack victims.

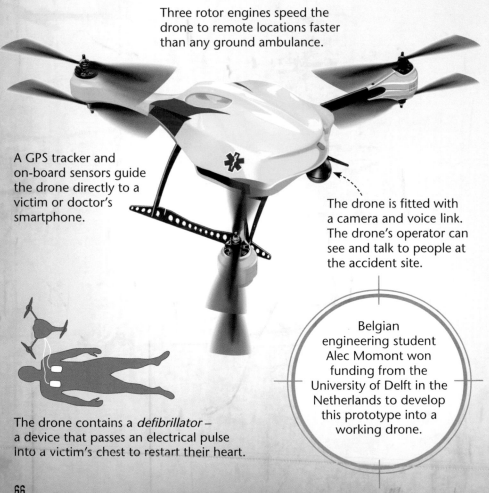

Three rotor engines speed the drone to remote locations faster than any ground ambulance.

A GPS tracker and on-board sensors guide the drone directly to a victim or doctor's smartphone.

The drone is fitted with a camera and voice link. The drone's operator can see and talk to people at the accident site.

Belgian engineering student Alec Momont won funding from the University of Delft in the Netherlands to develop this prototype into a working drone.

The drone contains a *defibrillator* – a device that passes an electrical pulse into a victim's chest to restart their heart.

Bouncy ball

This camera drone, known as *Gimball*, is housed inside a flexible sphere that was inspired by the way insects recover from bumps and collisions.

The lightweight orb can crash down stairs, off walls and even knock into people without causing hurt or damage.

Clean seas

This sail-powered drone, named *Protei*, is being developed to help clean oil spills at sea. Sailing in teams of thousands, each pulls a long, thick 'tail' that absorbs oil.

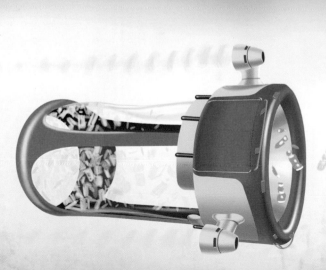

This self-guiding container, named *Marine Drone*, could one day swallow up plastic waste as it skims just below the surface of the water.

Learning from nature

By emulating the tricks and methods used by animals in motion, engineers are creating drones with special abilities. A machine that borrows ideas from nature is described as *bio-inspired*.

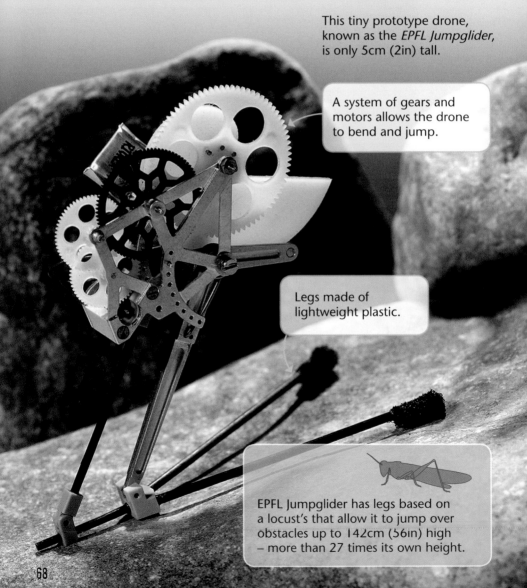

This tiny prototype drone, known as the *EPFL Jumpglider*, is only 5cm (2in) tall.

A system of gears and motors allows the drone to bend and jump.

Legs made of lightweight plastic.

EPFL Jumpglider has legs based on a locust's that allow it to jump over obstacles up to 142cm (56in) high – more than 27 times its own height.

Crossing new ground

Robots can't always get across surfaces that are too bumpy or too smooth. Engineers look to nature to help solve this kind of problem.

Under development at Carnegie Mellon University in the US is the *snake robot* – a drone that can slither up and down slopes, across sand and rubble, crawl through cracks and even climb trees.

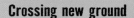

Linked segments, known as *modules*, allow the drone to twist and curl.

Cameras and lights at the fronts show what the drone can see.

Drone school

In special laboratory testing rooms, engineers push drones to their limits with no fear of them crashing into hard walls or floors.

Mapping thin air

The entire testing room is monitored by cameras and a computer that plots the exact location of each drone. The drones use this information to avoid obstacles and fly in complex formations.

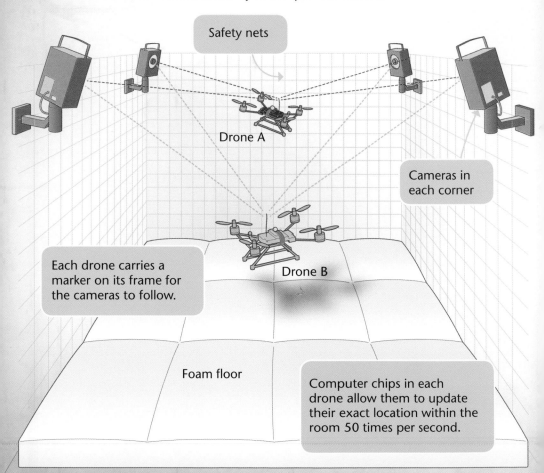

Safety nets

Drone A

Cameras in each corner

Each drone carries a marker on its frame for the cameras to follow.

Drone B

Foam floor

Computer chips in each drone allow them to update their exact location within the room 50 times per second.

Acrobatics

Using super fast processors, specially designed drones can check and correct their movements to perform some breathtaking stunts.

Obstacle course

This drone can identify and measure hoops to fly through them safely – even when the hoops are spinning.

Playing with poles

These two quadrotors are learning how to balance, throw and catch a pole. The pole has markers that the cameras can follow.

2 By flying straight up, then quickly pulling down, the drone can throw the pole.

1 Cameras track tiny movements on the pole markers, adjusting the drone to keep the pole balanced upright.

3 A second drone plots the trajectory of the pole as it spins and moves into position to catch it.

Teamwork

Drones with different sensors and abilities can work together to overcome challenges that would leave a single drone helpless.

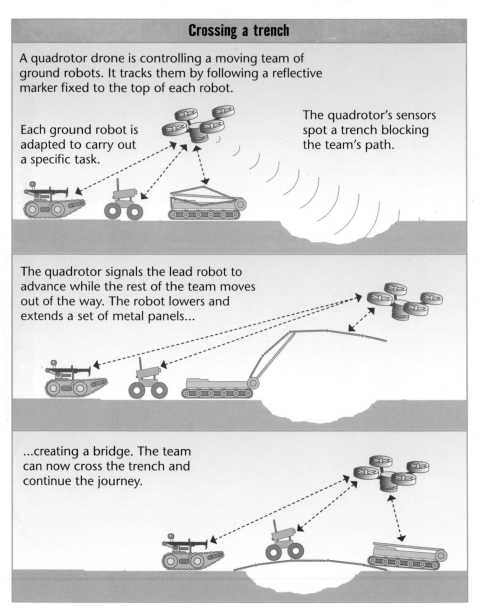

Crossing a trench

A quadrotor drone is controlling a moving team of ground robots. It tracks them by following a reflective marker fixed to the top of each robot.

Each ground robot is adapted to carry out a specific task.

The quadrotor's sensors spot a trench blocking the team's path.

The quadrotor signals the lead robot to advance while the rest of the team moves out of the way. The robot lowers and extends a set of metal panels...

...creating a bridge. The team can now cross the trench and continue the journey.

Engineers are developing minidrones that can roll or fly together in vast teams known as *swarms*.

These coin-sized drones are called *kilobots*, because they travel in teams of up to 1,000 individual drones.

In the future, drone swarms could be used to clean houses and city streets, or to build and repair damaged buildings.

Each individual kilobot is in constant contact with the drones closest to it. By communicating in small clusters, the whole swarm can combine to move in the same direction, or to build up complex shapes.

This illustration imagines a swarm of surveillance drones flying high over Los Angeles, providing constant video coverage of the city.

Busy skies

As more UAVs appear over our towns and cities, aviation experts and security agencies are calling for new laws and tests for drone pilots. UAVs offer fresh possibilities, but only if governments can safeguard public safety and privacy.

Questions raised

Problems	Solutions
1. Hack attack A computer hacker may be able to break into the radio codes used by UAV operators, and hijack control of a UAV in the air.	Stronger radio and software encryption is a top priority for UAV designers.
2. Pilot problems UAV sensors allow pilots to see even in fog and darkness – but in clear skies, nose cameras give a very narrow view compared to the pilot's view in a manned aircraft.	Adding more cameras to a drone builds up an ever-wider view – but none yet matches a pilot's eye view.
3. Target practice In the USA alone, many UAVs have been shot down by angry citizens who feel that UAV operators are infringing on their right to privacy.	Aviation laws make it illegal to fly drones too close to populated areas. In time, nearly all UAVs will need to be registered with police – like cars – so operators who break the law can be traced.
4. Moral safeguards Using drones does not risk the lives of the operators. Many people fear this means generals are quick to order drone strikes without thinking fully about the consequences.	International rules need to be established to decide when it is morally and legally acceptable to use unmanned vehicles and weapons.

This prototype drone, known as *GL-10 Greased Lightning*, is taking off during a test flight.

A larger model of the *Greased Lightning* would be able to carry several passengers or heavy cargo.

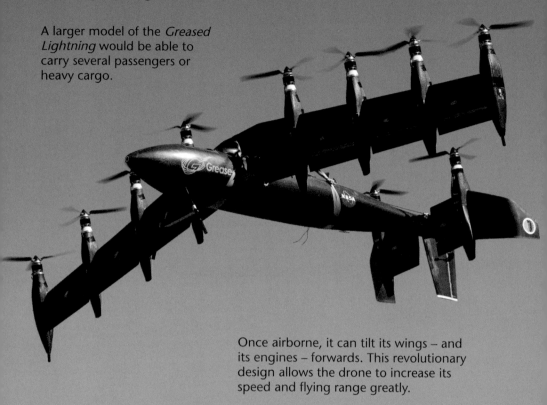

Once airborne, it can tilt its wings – and its engines – forwards. This revolutionary design allows the drone to increase its speed and flying range greatly.

Unmanned future

UAVs are flying faster, further and more safely than ever before. Some aviation experts believe unmanned machines will eventually replace the piloted aircraft that carry goods and passengers around our world – although for the time being, a human pilot will always be able to take control.

Glossary

This glossary explains some of the words used in this book. If a word is written in *italic* type, it has an entry of its own.

altimeter A device or sensor that records the height from the ground.

AUV Autonomous Underwater Vehicle, a marine drone that can operate at sea under its own power and navigation system.

drone Any unmanned vehicle, usually capable of flight, guided by a human operator or using its own on-board sensors and guidance system.

empennage The fins that make up the tail of an aircraft.

fireship A burning ship that was launched to collide with enemy ships, spreading fire as a weapon.

FPV First Person View, the camera link between a drone and its pilot.

fuselage The body or hull of an aircraft.

GCS Ground Control Station, a cabin with the screens, radio links and controls needed to operate a *drone*.

gimbal A rotating ball that can hold objects inside, such as a *gyroscope* or an array of cameras and sensors.

gyroscope A device used to measure movement, angle and direction.

kilobot A *nanodrone* that belongs to a *swarm* of one thousand machines.

MAV Micro Air Vehicle, a *drone* small enough to fit in a person's hand. Sometimes called microdrones.

missile A self-propelled weapon that can follow a guidance system.

nanodrone Any drone even smaller than an *MAV*.

quadcopter or **quadrotor** *UAVs* with four propeller engines.

radar Radio equipment that can detect moving objects and measure their speed, size and direction.

robot Any machine that carries out a complex series of tasks by itself.

rover A *robot* that can move along the ground.

swarm A collection of *nanodrones* or *MAVs* working together.

tether A rope, cable or radio signal that holds a hovering UAV in place.

UAV Unmanned Aerial Vehicle, another name for a flying *drone*.

UCAS Unmanned Combat Air System, another name for *UCAVs*.

UCAV Unmanned Aerial Combat Vehicle, a weaponized *drone*.

V-tails Sloping stabilizer fins in the tail assembly of an aircraft.

Index

Drones on the internet

For links to websites where you can watch videos of drones in action and see clips captured by drone cameras, from the view above an active volcano to exploring the surface of Mars, go to the Usborne Quicklinks website at **www.usborne.com/quicklinks** and enter the keyword: **drones**.

Usborne Publishing is not responsible and does not accept liability for the availability or content of any website other than its own, or for any exposure to harmful, offensive or inaccurate material which may appear on the Web. Usborne Publishing will have no liability for any damage or loss caused by viruses that may be downloaded as a result of browsing the sites it recommends.

Acknowledgements

Every effort has been made to trace and acknowledge ownership of copyright. If any rights have been omitted, the publishers offer to rectify this in any future editions following notification. The publishers are grateful to the following individuals and organizations for permission to feature and reproduce material on the following pages:

cover Parrot *AR.Drone 2.0* © Parrot; **p1** Parrot *Minidrone Jumping Sumo* © Parrot; **p2-3** courtesy AeroVironment, Inc; **p4** courtesy of General Atomics; **p10-11** © Erik Simonsen / Getty Images, with thanks to Northrop Grumman; **p12-13** with thanks to Flightglobal and Northrop Grumman; **p14-15** © Nigel Roddis / Getty Images; **p16** Seabattle at Solebay, 7th June 1672 by Willem van de Velde (the Younger). The National Maritime Museum, Amsterdam; **p19** © Imperial War Museum / H10307; **p21** © Detlev Van Ravenswaay / Science Photo Library; **p26-27** © Picture Alliance / Photoshot; **p28** © Ethan Miller / Getty Images; **p30-31** © 617 Collection / Alamy; **p32-33** with thanks to General Atomics, Northrop Grumman and BAE Systems; **p36** with thanks to QinetiQ UK; **p38-39** © Xinhua / Photoshot; **p42-43** © AFP / Getty Images; **p44-45** © Arnd Wiegmann / Reuters / Corbis; **p48** © Stocktrek Images, Inc. / Alamy; **p52** with thanks to Lockheed Martin; **p53** with thanks to NASA; **p54** © Ragnar Th. Sigurðsson / Arctic Images; **p55** © Eric Cheng | http://echeng.com; **p56** © US Air Force Photo / Alamy; **p60-61** courtesy of Mirko Kovac, Imperial Robotics Lab; **p62-63** with thanks to AeroVironment, Inc; **p64** © Prox Dynamics; **p66** with thanks to Alec Momont; **p67** (top) with thanks to Flyability SA; **p68** courtesy of Mirko Kovac, Imperial Robotics Lab; **p69** Photograph provided courtesy of Carnegie Mellon University; **p73** Photo by Mike Rubenstein, Harvard University; **p74-75** © John Lund / Blend Images / Corbis; **p76** © NASA.

Comic strips enhanced by Len O'Grady
Additional illustrations by Adrian Mann, Anna Gould and Helen Edmonds
Additional design by Alice Reece
Series editor: Jane Chisholm   Series designer: Zoe Wray
Digital design by John Russell   Picture research by Ruth King